12184

HENRI MATISSE

BY JEAN SELZ

CROWN PUBLISHERS, INC. · NEW YORK

Title page : PORTRAIT OF HENRI MATISSE BY ANDRÉ DERAIN, 1905
Oil 22″ × 15″
Tate Gallery, London

Translated from the French by :

A. P. H. HAMILTON

PRINTED IN ITALY

STILL LIFE WITH BOOKS AND CANDLE, 1890   Oil $8\frac{1}{2}'' \times 10\frac{1}{2}''$ Musée Matisse, Nice

A RESOLVE TO PAINT

I have arranged on my table some thirty pictures of Matisse. Some are old photographs and others were taken during the last few years of his life and show him sitting beside his dog or in his studio, working on a portrait of a model. There are also some reproductions of self-portraits in pencil, charcoal, or in Indian ink. There is a photo of him taken in about 1900. He has an impressive light-coloured beard, wears pince-nez glasses and there is a thoughtful, inquiring look in his expression, so characteristic of him later on when old age brought greater depth and serenity to an already grave face. Some self-portrait line-drawings combine precision and humour and leave behind a glimpse of delicacy in

Nude Leaning on Her Hand   Indian Ink 8″ × 10″   Metropolitan Museum of Art, New York

his expression with the trace of a smile beneath his glasses, suggesting a mischievous nature behind that serious, almost learned look. This is repeated in other pictures of Matisse as an old man, with a short white beard, reminiscent of Pasteur or Socrates.

There is the inescapable look of a calm, thoughtful man combining an apparently unshakable will and a characteristic resistance to outside influence. Pictures of Matisse reveal a man of truly independent ideas.

He was not only one of those rare artists of this century whose work defies any attempt at classification within a school; but, rarer still among artists, he refused to tie himself down exclusively to a particular style of painting. This explains why Matisse was not a theorist despite his skill in debating aesthetic subjects, and all that he said and wrote about painting, portraiture, drawing and colour. He enjoyed pondering over problems concerning his work, explaining his point of view and how he expressed what he saw. He talked and wrote about his relationship with nature, explaining the demands that his own view of art made on him. But his writings do not reveal him as a born teacher nor could his views on painting be considered as a text-book on art. The fact is that he mistrusted other peoples' theories and, as will be seen later, every time he experimented along certain lines which, early on, had assured him recognition by a particular school, he soon discarded all ready-made ideas because he was convinced that the direction he was to follow was for him and him alone.

Fortunately, Matisse, a man of very independent ideas, could draw upon a degree of will-power to match his independence, and proved that he could when he decided to devote his life to art in spite of the fact that, temperamentally and socially, he was hardly cut out for the career of an artist.

Henri Matisse was born on the 31st of December, 1869 at Cateau, in the department of the Nord, the son of a grain merchant with a shop at Bohain-en-Vermondois. He spent his childhood and school days at Bohain and later at Saint-Quentin until 1887 when his father sent him to Paris to study for a law examination. He returned the following year without having visited a single art gallery and took a job as clerk to a solicitor at Saint-Quentin, Maître Duconseil. At the age of twenty, Matisse showed no real interest in art, and although he showed a " certain ability " in drawing at his lycée, he had no idea that art would, one day, lead him away from the legal career that his family had chosen for him.

During his convalescence after an appendicitis operation, his neighbour in hospital spent his time copying coloured reproductions. This gave Matisse the idea of asking his mother to buy him a paint box. Matisse must have been sufficiently pleased with his first landscape of a river and a mill, for he signed it " Essitam ", his own name written in reverse. His experience in hospital resulted in his taking lessons at L'Ecole Quentin-Latour from a pupil of Bonnat. Before going to his office, Matisse spent an hour each day at the school. On Sundays, he visited the museums in the towns in the Nord and Pas-de-Calais departments and, in particular, the museum at Lille where he cannot have failed to see the still lifes by Jacob van Es and pictures by Rubens, the *Vieille fileuse* by Chardin, and the Goyas. This is how, relatively late in life, he began an education in art to which he was soon to devote himself entirely with an almost uncontrollable desire to learn.

The Matisse Museum, founded in January, 1963, and housed in the Villa des Arènes at Cimiez, above Nice, contains an amusing and clumsy little picture entitled *Book and Candle*. Studiously realist and painted in dark colours, it has something in common with 17th century Dutch still lifes. It was his first work of art, painted in 1890, and reveals the extent to which the painter developed over a period of more than fifty years. Since no one, apart from the artist himself, could forecast the future, it is all the more surprising that Matisse, against his father's wishes, abandoned an assured career he had prepared for himself on

Model. Around 1900 Pen and Ink
J. K. Thannhauser Gallery

the strength of this picture alone, and that he was to obey the irresistible force within him which drove him on to the less assured career of a painter.

Matisse arrived in Paris in October 1892 and registered for evening classes at the Ecole des Arts Décoratifs. Soon he was to enter the Académie Julian and the studio belonging to the most conventional painter of his time, William Bouguereau.

· STYLES AND TECHNIQUES

A painter's life story is important only insofar as it illustrates his artistic development. Conversely, his work is often created apparently without reference to the kind of life he led. Events in the life of Matisse have some bearing on his output but it is through his paintings that we approach Matisse, the man; without losing sight of the fact that an area of mystery always separates an artist from his work. The technical developments and changes in the style of work of most painters follow chronologically, with the result that their work is grouped according to styles and periods. This did not occur in the case of Matisse and one of the most perplexing aspects of his work is the ease with which he was able to pass from one style to another; from a realist's representation of relief in which the play of light and shade was obtained by using traditional perspective, to the presentation of surfaces on which flat tints did away with all notion of volume; finally, returning abruptly to a more classical conception, followed, for brief moments, by bold representations of geometrical forms.

We cannot, therefore, think in terms of periods when discussing Matisse. They did not develop logically, except very early on in his career, and until he had developed his own style.

The differences between his various styles are important and have a bearing on all his avenues of expression both in his selection and use of colours and his drawing technique. The following six pictures are so different that if nothing were known of the character and skill of Matisse there would be every reason for thinking that they were the work of different painters. There is no apparent similarity in style and technique between them

CYRANO, PORTRAIT OF LUCIEN GUITRY, 1903   Oil 31 ¾″ × 23 ½″
Mr and Mrs William Paley Collection, New York

NOTRE DAME, 1906   Oil 11¾″ × 12½″
Madame Ginette Signac Collection, Paris

WOMAN WITH PARASOL, 1905   Oil 18″ × 13¾″
Musée Matisse, Nice

10

Henri Matisse

Young Girl Reading or Marguerite Reading, 1906   Oil 25 1/4″ × 35 1/2″
Musée des Beaux Arts, Grenoble

◁

Woman with Hat, 1905   Oil 32″ × 25 1/2″
Mr and Mrs Walter A. Haas Collection, San Francisco

PORTRAIT WITH GREEN STRIPE, 1905   Oil 16″ × 12³/₄″
J. Rump Collection, Royal Museum of Fine Arts, Copenhagen

SELF-PORTRAIT OF THE ARTIST WITH JERSEY, 1906   Oil 21¾″ × 18″
J. Rump Collection, Royal Museum of Fine Arts, Copenhagen

MADAME MATISSE, 1913   Oil 58″×38¼″   Hermitage Museum, Leningrad

— *The Breton Weaver* (1896), *Study, Saint Tropez* (1904), *Woman with Hat* (1905), *Head, White and Rose* (1915), *Odalisque in Red Trousers* (1922), and *Dancer Sitting in an Armchair* (1942) contains something of the style of Corot and Chardin. Every technique used in this work, from the touch of monotony in the refined harmony of the ochre and grey-green tints, the studied, careful drawing and balanced composition, had already been developed by other painters. It reveals that Matisse, at the outset was still influenced by what he had learnt at school and seen in the galleries he visited. The second, *Study, Saint Tropez* (Madame Ginette Signac's Collection, Paris) is pure neo-impressionism. The stipple technique is there with its juxtapositions of pure colour tones as recommended by Signac and his followers. In *Woman with Hat* (Walter A. Haas's Collection, San Francisco) separate colour splashes no longer appear, and the work is representative of fully developed Fauvism with its wide brush

Study for "White Plumes", 1919   Lead Pencil

strokes and bright colours which caused such an uproar at the never to be forgotten Salon d'Automne of 1905 at which this picture was exhibited. Liberty gives place to the discipline of harsh and strict geometry, born of Cubism, in the portrait of Madame Matisse, *Head, White and Rose* (Jean Matisse's Collection, Pontoise). On the other hand, *Odalisque in Red Trousers* (Musée National d'Art Moderne in Paris) painted seven years later and boldly aesthetic, appears to represent a return to a more classical idea of form.   The colour has moderated and become more fluid, and the subject, most carefully depicted, particularly the body of the Odalisque, reveals a degree of realism absent from the three previous pictures.   Finally, in *Dancer Sitting in an Armchair* (Madame Marcel Duchamp Collection, New York) both shadow and relief have disappeared.   The five colours appearing in the picture, flat tints, partly delimited by an outline, appear to be quite free of any association with conventional volume.

These last two styles predominate, alternatively, in the works of Matisse.   The contrast between the two styles and techniques are, in fact, keys to an understanding of his creative spirit.   It explains the duality resulting from his desire to depict nature accurately and his need to escape from it. A side of his character is revealed as well: a desire never to upset the balance which made him hesitate between a very rational taste for moderation and an overwhelming desire to revolt.

To understand how this contradiction originated and found expression, it is necessary to return to his early years as a painter. Apart from *The Weaver* there are a few other paintings of 1896 *The Swineherd* (Musée Matisse at Cimiez), *Still Life with a Black Knife, Interior with a Top Hat, Rocks at Belle Ile,* the portrait of *Nini Pétron,* and the relatively unknown *Still Life with Grapes* (David Rockfeller Collection). These were painted when Matisse

LANDSCAPE AT COLLIOURE (Study for " Bonheur de vivre "), 1905
J. Rump Collection, Royal Museum of Fine Arts, Copenhagen

SIESTA OR INTERIOR AT COLLIOURE, 1905   Oil 23 ½″ × 28 ¾″   Private Collection, Ascona

had been working for a year in Gustave Moreau's studio where he had gone to escape from the boredom at Bouguearau's. Thanks to Moreau, he had managed to be accepted at L'Ecole des Beaux Arts without having to pass the entrance examination.

All these pictures belong to what is called his old style, or more accurately, his old styles on account of the noticeable absence of unity and, compared with *Books and Candle* (1890) and even *Woman Reading* of 1895 (Musée National d'Art Moderne in Paris) they show clearly that he had matured articulately. There was more precision in his composition and a surer touch in his workmanship.

It is clear that what Matisse had learnt from Gustave Moreau was a vital factor in his mas-

19

tery over his problems as an artist. Moreau's special interest in mythical adventure, a mania for affectation and his symbolism were entirely alien to Matisse. But he never involved his pupils in a style that was peculiar to him but made a point of encouraging them to develop their art as they felt inclined. He encouraged them to improve their knowledge of the Great Masters and to take an interest in all forms of contemporary art. The result was that all who worked with him, Rouault, Desvallières, Camoin, Manguin, Piot, Evènepoel, and later on, Marquet, with whom Matisse had become very friendly when they met at the Ecole des Arts Décoratifs, recognised that Moreau was an outstanding teacher.

Matisse regularly visited the Louvre and made many copies of works of art during the three years he spent at Moreau's studio from 1895 to 1898, the year of Moreau's death. He continued to visit the Louvre until 1900. He studied a great variety of artists' works, among them David de Heem, Raphael, Poussin, Ruysdael, Carrache, Boucher, Fragonard, Watteau, Ribera, Delacroix, and in particular, Chardin. This sustained effort was due more to his desire to discover how these painters had solved the problem of values with which Matisse was then wrestling than to any eclectic element in his tastes.

Chardin's influence on Matisse was responsible for his paintings of subjects bathed in soft light, interiors and still lifes. Matisse made copies of five of Chardin's works, one of which, bought by the French State, is exhibited at the Town Hall in Grenoble. Chardin's influence on Matisse is to be found in many paintings of this period and it is possible to follow closely the progress he made towards a freer use of the brush and a less conventional use of colour. *Woman Reading*, dark in colour with a not very successful use of ochre and red brown dominant tints was an example of laboured and not very outstanding brushwork. The colour tones in the portrait of *Nini Pétron* are still inclined to be dull, but rather more refined. But in *Rocks at Belle Ile* Matisse made a great use of bright colour to satisfy his desire to concentrate on painting masses rather than detail.

Matisse had shown little interest in landscape painting until 1896 when, on holiday in the summer at Belle-Ile, he met John Russel, an Australian artist and friend of Monet who introduced him to Impressionism. Matisse did not, then, become interested in this new style since he was, by nature, slow to accept ideas he had not, himself, put to the test. He was, at this stage, more attracted to the strict precision and brilliance of Manet's style than to the diffused light on canvases by Monet and other impressionists which seemed, to him, unnecessarily untidy. He had, in any case, not yet shown signs of being the brilliant colourist that he was to become, though, in some of his pictures, he was showing a greater freedom of expression in both composition and choice of colour.

He worked on, stubbornly conscientious, with a determination to see through to the end, a study he had deliberately undertaken, and to decide, finally, upon the style he was to adopt in the light of the results of his experiments, patiently undertaken. It was in this frame of mind that, in 1897, Matisse exhibited at the Salon of the Société Nationale des Beaux-Arts for the second year running. His contribution was a large canvas, *Dinner Table* with which he hoped to make his influence felt. This intimate portrait showed a servant

THE DESSERT OR HARMONY IN RED, 1908   Oil $69\frac{3}{4}'' \times 85\frac{3}{4}''$
Hermitage Museum, Leningrad

THE DANCE, 1910
Oil 102¹/₂″ × 154″
Hermitage Museum
Leningrad
▷

MUSIC, 1910
Oil 102¹/₂″ × 153¹/₂″
Hermitage Museum
Leningrad
▷

BOY WITH BUTTERFLY NET, 1907   Oil 69″ × 44¹/₄″
Institute of Art, Minneapolis, USA

GIRL IN GREEN DRESS, 1909   Oil 25½″×21¼″   Hermitage Museum, Leningrad

24

leaning over a table already laid, arranging flowers in a vase. Dishes of fruit, jugs of wine and crystal glasses on the white table cloth prove a still life which the painter had composed with all the care he could lavish upon it. The dominant ochre and brown tints recalled the harmony of his earlier works, but the unexpected off-whiteness of the tablecloth, the intensity of some orange tints, the carefully executed colours of some shadows, and the angle at which the table is seen from above, are proof of a further development, only moderately impressionist, but a definite step towards a new " modernist " technique.

Dinner Table was not so successful as Matisse had hoped. He was disappointed, but was not one to be discouraged by so sudden a disappointment, nor did he relax the tempo of his experiments. Proof of this is found in the pictures painted the following year when he travelled with his wife to Corsica in 1898, the year of his marriage. He was now able to apply a form of expression that he had only partly studied in theory.

Matisse, the northerner, was on the threshold of a wealth of discoveries in the Mediterranean world with its superb climate and exceptional light. The joy he experienced was to appear again and again in his paintings until the end of his career. He wrote to Raymond Escholier — " It was in Ajaccio that I found my joy and affection for the south ". His Corsican paintings, *Room in Ajaccio* (from a private collection), *The Invalid* (Baltimore Museum, Cone Collection) represent the first attempt to treat his choice of colour on an equal footing with his draughtsmanship. In the two works, and more particularly in *The Sick Woman* of a woman in bed, there is no hint of an intimate treatment of the subject. There is no sign of careful attention to detail as was scrupulously observed in *The Sick Woman* The actual forms took second place to a portrayal of mass; colours generously distributed with a grouping of colour ranges. The general effect created by this technique was akin to Impressionism.

There was a touch of effeminacy in this technique which cannot have satisfied Matisse. Although he persisted with his notion of simplifying the representation of volume, he showed in *Village in the Midi, Street in Arcueil* (The Copenhagen Museum) painted the following year, that he was capable of a more vigorous composition in which the plane surfaces of walls and ground, light and shade created geometrical patterns. It is also possible that his admiration for Cézanne, from whom he had bought a small work of art and whom he called " the great god of painting ", may have encouraged him to pay stricter attention to his draughtsmanship. But his great achievement at this time was the discovery that a wider use of colour lay within his grasp. Now that he had acquired a great depth of feeling for colour, Matisse became Matisse.

Portrait of Serge Stchoukine, 1912   Charcoal $19^{1}/_{4}'' \times 11^{3}/_{4}''$

COLOUR UNLIMITED

Seven years elapsed between his paintings at Ajaccio and the first in the style of the Fauves. This period, between 1898 and 1905 may seem unduly long if it is thought that his style and technique developed logically. But Matisse advanced by devious routes and, especially during his experimental stage, advanced cautiously, never commiting himself to a particular course without being sure of himself. Some individual paintings, executed in a bolder style, contained techniques that he probably expected to return to later on, when he was certain that he was personally in tune with the new medium.

In the meantime, he had to continue studying so as to complete his apprenticeship. But, since the death, from cancer, of Gustave Moreau, on 18th April 1898, he had lost all interest in l'Ecole des Beaux-Arts. Cormon succeeded Moreau, but Matisse did not feel drawn to work with a new professor whose main interests were austere studies of prehistoric life. Matisse preferred to paint in the open air around Paris, alone, or with Marquet. He joined the Carrière studio, housed in small premises in the rue de Rennes where Derain also worked. Paintings of this period, such as *Nude Study* and *Nude in Pink Slippers* showed the care that Matisse took to reconcile a solid, overall construction of the picture with drawing bordering on the classical, and a more fanciful colour scheme with red and green flesh tones proclaiming the glitter of a still more restricted colour range of a later period.

Life had become more difficult for Matisse since the birth of his two sons, Jean in 1899, and Pierre in 1900. He found he had to adapt his own experiments to the need to earn more money by working for Jambon, a decorator, and by participating in the décor of the Grand Palais in Paris. He was put to work sketching interminable laurel friezes on the walls. He continued to exhibit annually at the Independents' from 1901 and at the Salon d'Automne from 1903. Dealers began to take a serious interest in his works, which were now found in Berthe Weill's gallery in 1902, Druet's in 1903, and Vollard's in 1904. He began studying sculpture, and two statuettes appear among his exhibits in the 1904 Salon d'Automne.

This was an important year for him. He spent the summer at Saint Tropez where he met Paul Signac and Henri Edmond Cross. He took full advantage of the bright Mediterranean sun to develop a new technique. Signac and Cross had taken a keen interest in the neo-Impressionist theories which they were practicing with what amounted to strict devotion. They held endless discussions and, rather than laying claim to an exclusive right to use this art form, they sought to convert Matisse to practise the technique of the separate dash of colour. Matisse, though not over-enthusiastic about so systematic a technique, nevertheless experimented without great success. He could not manage, completely, to give up his own style, and Signac recognised the difficulties that Matisse was meeting in adapting himself to the limitations imposed by a separation of colour.

*Portrait
of Mademoiselle
Eva Mudocci
1915
Charcoal* ·

MARGUERITE
MATISSE
GIRL WITH
A BLACK CAT
37″ × 25 ¹/₄″
Mrs. George
Duthuit
Collection, Paris

The important exhibition of works by Signac at Druet's in December 1904, with Felix Fénéon's preface to the catalogue, saw the end of the public's indifference to the new style. There followed a burst of public enthusiasm for the seascapes and views of Venice in which pure colour tones lay side by side with limpid and harmonious shades of light. Then, for a few months, Matisse set to work on that mosaic-like technique. The picture which best illustrates this style is *Study, Saint Tropez* which was shown at the Independents' in 1905. The title, with its epicurean overtones, which Matisse developed further later on in his representation of a peaceful and happy world, denotes with equal emphasis a literary leaning which remained one of his outstanding characteristics. Matisse, however, never reached the same pitch of perfection achieved by recognised masters of the stipple technique. The geometrical and technical precision was not easily adaptable to supple forms of nudes on a red river bank. Matisse's determination to resist so trivial a process sprang once again from the fact that he was denied the ability to master it.

The methodical, yet hesitant way, in which Matisse translated a subject into neo-Impressionist language is no secret today. It is revealed in *Nude in Studio* (1905) now hanging in the Musée National d'Art Moderne in Paris. This picture shows Marquet painting in Manguin's studio. The first version of this subject is a gouache in which colour and draughtsmanship are happily married and there is no stipple. The second version in oils shows small rectangular brush strokes. It is clear that Matisse had some difficulty in mastering the change from one technique to another. The same can be said about the two versions of *Still Life with a Purro* painted at Saint-Tropez in which the second is a stippled transformation of the first. This picture is now in the collection of Mr and Mrs John Hay Whitney of New York.

Matisse soon freed his style from these restrictions. In *Pastoral* (Musée d'Art Moderne de la Ville de Paris) there are clear signs that the new-Impressionist style contains traces of Fauvism. Unlike those artists aware of the possibility of fragmenting rich colour, Matisse used pure colour tones in a different way. Even though Signac's exhibition had drawn Matisse towards the technique of stippling, it appears that it was the combined Seurat and Van Gogh exhibits at the 1905 Independents' which caused Matisse to break away. Did Matisse realise how far ahead Seurat was of other artists using the stipple technique and that Seurat had added style to a technique that appeared no more than an art process when practised by Signac, and that this process would lead him to a dead end? Moreover, the example of Van Gogh who had made great strides in what might be called the putting of colour into motion by his nervous, animated brushwork, betokening a tortured mind, could not fail to attract the attention of Matisse. The mastery and power of his art towered over the innocuous geometry of the small coloured rectangles. Matisse was, by nature, too liberal minded to allow himself to be held prisoner by what amounted to a system.

The summer he spent at *Collioure* with Derain produced a distinct but gradual change in Matisse. Some paintings of the region still show signs of stipple technique, but the independence that developed in his Fauvist period had begun to break out.

30

Seated Nude, 1936 Pen and Indian Ink

ZORA. THE YELLOW DRESS. Tangiers, 1912   Oil 32 × 25¼"   Private Collection, Chicago, USA

Matisse, one of the first Fauvists, was now fast fulfilling all his earlier promise as his art came to fruition, free of any doctrinal influence. There were signs, however, especially in *Lux, Calme and Volupté*, that he had not yet completely solved the problem of the assimilation of flat tints in the representation of volume and the conception of space. But already his passionate arrangement of colour in which vermilion full-bloodedly clashes with green, reveals that something more important than the representation of space and volume has leapt into Matisse's vision. The almost frenzied use of pure colours announced a new spiritual approach and revealed both a refusal to accept convention in his energetic application and a reappraisal of the art of painting. His outlook at the time can be summed up by his observation " Fauvism is found only where there is courage to revert to utter purity of execution ".

One other curious phenomenon of the Fauvist movement distinguishing it from all others brought into being by the Impressionists, neo-Impressionists, Nabis and Cubists, is that it is not based on theory. It was not entirely by chance that several artists began, simultaneously, to paint in similar styles and it would be pointless to try to find out who it was who introduced the movement. A fusion of minds, ideas and tastes with a free flow of influence brought into being by the warmth of friendships, a kind of complicity bordering on provocation, was the origin of this shared aesthetic creation. None of those involved was able to provide a satisfactory explanation since none of them was a theorist; indeed the forces that brought men of such different ideas together, such as Matisse, Vlaminck and Marquet, was their common hostility to the theoretical approach to art. Perhaps the Fauvist " scandal " would not have been such an immediate success and the origin of such a powerful movement, if the 1905 Salon d'Automn had not exhibited together in room VII, works by Matisse, Derain, Vlaminck, Manguin, Valtat and others; proud champions of pure colour; and if their association had not been declared a coalition threatening the very future of contemporary art.

It is possible that the fact that there was so little exchange of idealogical opinions was the main reason why the Fauvist movement lasted three short years, coming to an end as it did with the dispersal of its members whose individual interests in art finally saw them go their own separate ways.

For Matisse alone, the vivid exultation that Fauvism brought was something more than the temporary satisfaction of a desire for freedom of expression. He continued to draw upon certain aspects of Fauvism on a tighter rein and remained faithful to the use of pure colour, abandoning it at intervals only to return again with a renewed freshness, possessed as he was with a youthfulness that remained with him until the end of his days.

In periods of exultation, Matisse remained essentially a thinker. This is borne out even in mighty works of art painted between 1905 and 1907 at the height of his Fauvist period. In *Woman with Hat* where there is a frenzied use of colour, each tone seems to call out more loudly than its neighbour, the distribution of warm and cold colours and the accentuated dark shades in the dress offset the colours applied to the central feature,

The Artist and His Model, 1937   Pen and Indian Ink

the hat. In spite of the violence of contrasted colour, the composition reveals that Matisse was applying a classical sense of balance between colour masses.

In *The Siesta (Interior in Collioure)* in which a woman, wearing a green dress, is lying on a pink bed, the floor of the room is red and the three chairs against the wall are partly in shadow and partly in the sun. Through the open window, a little girl can be seen on the terrace, wearing a red dress and contemplating the countryside about her. A feeling of warmth comes out from the picture, but the whole length of the wall, a large area of green and blue shadow, separates the bed from the window as though it were a boundary line between the deep sleep of the recumbent woman and the warmth of the Provinçale afternoon. The simplicity of the artist's technique, the colours spread thinly over large areas of the picture, the impression that the intensity of the sun, the silence and the stillness are responsible for the complete absence of relief, that all objects are floating, powerless under the hot sun and the woman asleep, all combine to suggest that, in spite of its spontaneity, this is a picture which Matisse had long contemplated and savoured in his imagination.

There are other works, such as *Gipsy*, painted in 1906 (Musée de l'Annonciade, Saint Tropez), in which the energy and rapidity of the brushwork stand out and the picture is so completely filled with spontaneity and life, that a prolonged study of the model seems out of the question. Colour takes precedence and forms do not necessarily bear close resemblance to the original. Green, red, yellow and orange unite to create a mottled effect upon the face and naked bust of the witch. At the time, this treatment of a subject must have struck the public as a challenge to the recognised representation of form.

In *Young Girl Reading* (Musée des Beaux Arts, Grenoble) a portrait of the artist's daughter Marguerite, painted in 1906, the same year as *Gipsy*, we find a more restrained Matisse, far removed from the reckless Fauve of the same period. The little girl is dressed in red with her black hair tumbling down her back. She is sitting at a table, leaning on an elbow, her face buried in a book. In this picture, the drawing conforms to the laws of composition with the forms almost ringed around, apparently in an effort to resist the vagrant brush. The colours are, on the whole, sober and unhurriedly painted, though in places they show up in a lively light.

It is now becoming clear how, under the influence of Fauvism, Matisse was advancing towards a technique which was later to dominate much of his artistic output. He cut his range of colours down to a few vivid tones and was content with a minimum of forms all methodically thought out. Some forty years later, he was to say — " colours have a beauty all of their own and must be preserved, just as, in music, it is the timbre that must not be lost ". These two acquisitions, the outline and the flat tint, were to help him to work out his ideas on the independent nature of colour. But, in the meantime, though he broke free from traditional realism as regards colour, he realised that the use of flat tints and the absence of shadows left volume unexpressed. This is, perhaps, the reason why Matisse is seen to paint, alternatively, pictures such as *Landscape at Collioure* (Statens Museum for Kunst, Copenhagen) or *The Siesta* at a time when, with Derain, Vlaminck and Braque, he shared the notion of colour withdrawn from the representation of relief, and other pictures in which he tried to suggest relief by a partial return to the representation of shadow such as in *Blue Nude* (Museum of Art, Collection Cone, Baltimore) painted in 1907 to commemorate a visit to Biskera. A close study of this picture shows that Matisse was already searching for a means of expression, different from that found in the original Fauve technique. The woman, reclining on the grass, with palm trees in the background, is drawn with very noticeable and vigorous dark strokes of the pen. The shadows, tinted blue, occasionally in hachures, throws up the pink flesh tones.

In all the variations that Matisse introduced into his paintings at this period, because he refused to accept a ready-made and imposed formula, there is a sense of enrichment which cannot be overlooked, showing that his experience as a Fauve was of the greatest benefit to him as it was to most of the painters in the group. Whereas others in the group consi-

Portrait of a Woman
1938 Linoleum

dered the mastery of Fauvism as an accomplishment in itself, to be repeated, or renounced in favour of other art froms such as Cubism, for Matisse it constituted a valuable step in a new direction. When fully explored, and looked at in retrospect, Matisse's traces of fauvism are noticeable in much of his later art. In each important work by Matisse at this period, there are indications which reveal how active he was in his investigations. There are signs, too, of future developments. There is the strange portrait of *Madame Matisse*, 1905 (Statens Museum for Kunst, Copenhagen) in which the full face is traversed by a bright, green line running down the middle. Again in the still life, *Pink Onions*, 1906 (Statens Museum for Kunst, Copenhagen), a simple decorative work, the outline is absent and special importance is given to ornamental detail. The work, *Le Luxe* painted in 1907, a great and somewhat mysterious composition in which several techniques are mingled; outline, flat tints, a discreet representation of forms, and, across the sky, made up of little touches of mauve, passes, in profile, one of the three nudes in the picture. This work contains the first hesitant approach towards a technique in which forms are reduced to their simplest proportions. It was not until three years later, in 1910 that this notion was fully developed in *The Dance*. Matisse elected to prolong his Fauvist period after 1908, when the originators in France began to lose interest, though, outside France, artists such as Jawlensky, Kandinsky, Kirchner and Macke were late in accepting it. By concentrating upon details in his drawing, Matisse added calmness to his compositions and continued in the Fauvist tradition. His portraits, in which forms, without being geometrical, were reduced to their simplest expression and colour contrasts were restricted: — in 1908 *Red Madras Headdress* (Barnes Foundation, Merion, USA) in 1909 *Algerian Woman* (Musée National d'Art Moderne, Paris) and *Girl in Green Dress* (Musée de l'Ermitage, Leningrad); in 1910 *Girl with a Black Cat* (Madame Duthuit's Collection). These represent some of the post-Fauvist works of Matisse which will be studied in greater detail later on.

A rather clumsily painted picture, *The Dessert, Harmony in Red* (Musée de l'Ermitage, Le-

FLOWERS AND POTTERY, 1911 Oil 36½″×32½″ Formerly LeRay Berdeau Collection, Palm Beach, USA

PORTRAIT OF YVONNE
LANDSBERG, 1914
Oil 57$\frac{1}{2}$″ × 41$\frac{1}{4}$″
Museum of Art
Philadelphia

38   MARGUERITE MATISSE. HEAD WHITE AND ROSE, 1915   Oil 29$\frac{1}{4}$″ × 17$\frac{1}{4}$″
Jean Matisse Collection, Pontoise

LORETTE WITH BLACK BACKGROUND, 1916   Oil 28³/₄″ × 21¹/₂″
Owned by the Artist's Family

▷

40   THE ARTIST AND HIS MODEL, 1916   Oil 57³/₄″ × 38¹/₄″
                                          Musée National d'Art Moderne, Paris

◁
PEWTER JUG, 1916-1917   Oil 36¼″×25½″
Cone Collection, Museum of Art, Baltimore

MARGUERITE MATISSE, HEAD WITH BLACK VELVET, 1916
Oil 7″×6¾″   Owned by the Artist's Family

43

PINEAPPLE AND ANEMONIES, 1940   Oil $36\frac{1}{4}'' \times 28\frac{3}{4}''$
Mrs Albert D. Lasker Collection, New York

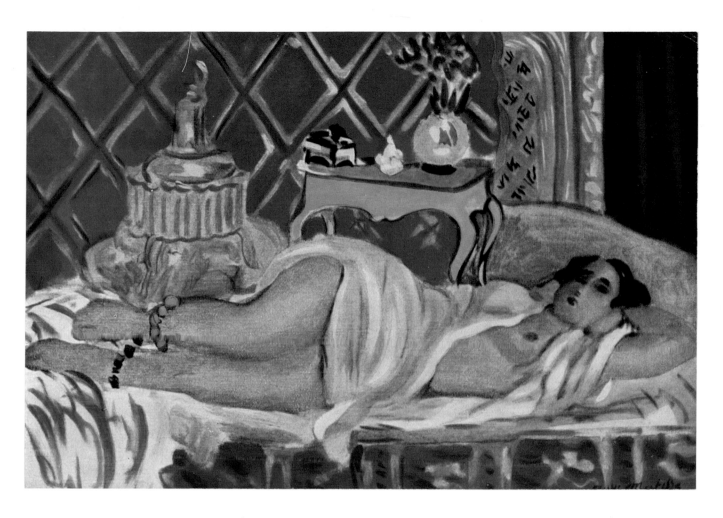

RED ODALISQUE, 1928   Oil 21 ¹/₂" × 15ʺ Private Collection, Paris

ningrad) dated 1908 already contained aesthetic principles which were later to be of absorbing interest to him.   There are no traces of the intimate realism characteristic of *Dinner Table*, painted in 1897, in which the servant is seen arranging a table bearing jugs and fruit dishes.   The green rectangle, representing the countryside through the open window, stands out in bold contrast, in one corner of the composition, to the mass of red filling the rest of the picture.   The figure of the servant, the objects on the table and the ornamental motifs on the carpet and the wall are all outlined in black and stand out in relief against the gleaming background.   What strikes the eye with an almost embarrassing effect are the ornamental motifs.   Of these, the blue arabesque entwined in the baroque style appear as the main subject of the picture.   This conception of an art form in which an essentially graphic theme predominates will be examined in greater detail later on.   It will appear in Matisse's works as one of the outstanding and haunting manifestations of his personality.   Apart from the vigorous treatment in *The Dessert, Harmony in Red*, all that need be noticed at

Seated Nude, 1930   Etching

this stage is that Matisse had accepted the flat tint technique and this was to occupy an important place in his output later on. Once again, in this picture, Matisse can be seen to predict how his painting is to develop in the future. Many other techniques, also, were to occupy his mind. Although at this time, Matisse was still being abused by critics with the exception of Marcel Sembat and Guillaume Apollinaire, whose articles on his painting contained unstinted praise, foreign art collectors were taking a serious interest in his work. The most interested of them was that curious family Stein; Gertrude and Leo, Michel and his wife Sarah, who were very active collectors where *avant-garde* art was concerned. Leo had already acquired *Woman with Hat* in 1905. His sister and he bought several paintings in 1906, the year in which Matisse showed forty-six of his works at Druet's, while Michel and Sarah bought *Pink Onions* and the fine *Self Portrait* in which the artist is dressed in a sailor's jersey. The following year, they bought *Still Life with Blue Cameo* (now in the Barnes Foundation at Merion). Every day, art dealers became increasingly interested in Matisse, whose output was now very considerable. He continued sculpturing, travelled in Italy in 1907, showed thirty works at the Salon d'Automne and stayed in Munich and Berlin, where he exhibited at Cassirer's. His pictures were to be found as far apart as London, Stockholm, Moscow and in the Gallery 291 of Alfred Stieglitz in New York. His prestige was beginning to grow. He signed a contract with Bernheim who took sixty-six pictures in 1910. The same year found him working on *The Dance* and *Music* commissioned by the collector Serge Stchoukine for his Moscow house. He had already bought *Harmony in Red* and was later to buy thirty-four other works which, to-day, are found in Moscow and Leningrad museums.

And now, Matisse, whose studio was in the old Convent des Oiseaux in the rue de Sèvres, opened an acadamy there. It was transferred in 1910 to a house at Issy-les-Moulinaux in another disused convent of Le Sacré Cœur in the Boulevard des Invalides, while Marquet took over his apartment on the Quai Saint-Michel in Paris. Young painters, many of them foreigners, Per Krogh, Feder, Czobel, Nils de Dardel and Marie Wassilief became his enthusiastic pupils at the new studio. After a year, Matisse, too busy with his own work, exhibitions and journeys, finally gave up his academy and in the same year made one famous trip to Moscow where he was the guest of Stchoukine.

Several months in 1912 were spent in Morocco, and he returned there in 1913. He spent much time making notes of what he saw, and these were to inspire many of his later pictures. In 1914, he returned to his studio in Paris at 19, Quai Saint-Michel. Invalided out of the army in September, he took up residence at Collioure with Marquet and Juan Gris. Much of the war was spent at Nice where he experimented in methods which were so new to him and different from hose associated with him, that it might be thought they were to announce a complete change in his artistic interests. These experimental pictures were, in fact, to remain unusual and rare examples of his art.

Portrait of Mademoiselle Claribel Cone, 1934
Charcoal Cone Collection, Museum of Art, Baltimore

Cubism had, for several years, overtaken Fauvism in the minds of *avant-garde* artists. Matisse was attracted for a time to Cubism as a more constructive means of expression and one which was to have a profound effect on his aesthetic sense. The portrait of *Mademoiselle Yvonne Landsberg* (Museum of Art, Philadelphia), painted in 1914, in somewhat dark colours, with grey tints varying between blue and violet, in browns and ochres, was very unlike Matisse's usual style, because the outline of forms using a system of curves are superimposed on the silhouette of the model. The hard features of the face have something of the look of a primitive wood carving which Picasso had given to his *Demoiselles d'Avignon*. The absence of curves in *Head, White and Rose*, a portrait of Marguerite Matisse, is due to the concentrated geometrical design of the picture. Areas of colour are broken up by a thick black line resembling leading in a stained glass window. *The Moroccans*, 1916 (Museum of Modern Art, New York) is almost incomprehensible, owing to the extent to which the areas of colour are reduced to their basic proportions, and with the purity of its conception, this work contains elements of what, later on, was to be called geometrical abstraction. *Bathers by a River*, 1916-1917 (Art Institute of Chicago), a rather more mysterious subject, has something in common with *The Moroccans*. It is a very large picture, measuring (12′8″ × 8′5″). Its various elements have little in common with each other though there is a measure of unity in the style which is purely decorative. The drawing has been simplified to the extent of eliminating the faces.

All these pictures are of the greatest interest. It is a pity that Matisse did not develop further a style in which he might have excelled, judged by the few furtive experiments in his pictures. But he was to discover his future destiny as a painter in different ways. Firstly, he was to depict nature as a realist in his series of *Odalisques* of which *Red Odalisque* of 1928 is an example of the painter's most " classicist " style. Secondly, he was to reduce forms to a few areas of colour without paying attention to the representation of relief, where the element of decoration remained paramount, and in the majority of cases he used bright colours (*Pink Nude*, painted in 1935, now at the Museum of Art, Collection Cone, Baltimore). The ageing Matisse was bent on showing that the bright lights of Fauvism were far from dim.

MATISSE, THE PAINTER OF PORTRAITS

" The subject matter I prefer to the still life or the landscape is the portrait. It enables me to express in the best possible way what might be called the religious feeling I have for life ". Matisse wrote these words in 1908. Would he still have felt the same way later on when his portraiture had lost its liveliness? Using various styles and techniques, his subject was usually feminine. There is a vast difference between the vivacity of his *Odalisques* and the portraits, lacking in personality, painted late in life when Matisse no longer depicted women, but dresses and corsets which clothed entirely abstract people. This was not due solely to the effect of a change in the way he portrayed forms, but was also an indication that he was no longer taking the same interest in the character of the model. Humanity, painted by Matisse, blossomed out in bright colours and the result was nothing more than a representation of plastic art.

Even in his moments of vivid realism, Matisse never lost sight of the importance of draughtsmanship and how it drew constituent parts of the picture together by an assimilation of the living subject to the requirements of the decor. In his nudes, sensuality is absent for the very good reason that he no longer considered it of sufficient interest. It was this fact that prompted Aragon to say — " Henri Matisse's drawing of a model, a woman or a flower, possesses enormous intellectual chastity ".

Matisse painted a great number of portraits without ever trying to employ the art of painting as a tool for psychological investigation. Some of his portraits are among his most remarkable works of art. What, then, was the reason for the variations in his aesthetic development as regards the portrayal of the human face?

DECORATIVE FIGURE ON ORNAMENTAL BACKGROUND, 1927 Oil 51″×38½″
Musée National d'Art Moderne, Paris

BLUE NUDE (Memory of Biskra), 1907   Oil 36¼" × 55"   Cone Collection, Museum of Art, Baltimore

PINK NUDE, 1935   Oil 26" × 36¾"   Cone Collection, Museum of Art, Baltimore

WOMAN WITH RED JACKET, 1937
Oil 21³/₄″ × 18¹/₄″ Paul Rosenberg Collection, Paris and New York

LARGE STUDIO, 1911   Oil 67$\frac{1}{2}$" × 87$\frac{3}{4}$"   Pushkin Museum, Moscow

In the preface to his collection of drawings and representations of his paintings entitled *Portraits* (André Sauret, Monte-Carlo, 1954) Matisse expressed his feelings about portraiture — " Portraiture is one of the oddest of the arts. It demands the possession of very special gifts by the artist and the ability to identify himself with his model ". The very particular nature of this identification will be understood only if the painter's vision is completed by something else Matisse once said, and which was recorded by André Verdet (*Prestiges de Matisse*: Emile-Paul 1952) " you begin to feel you are yourself only when you get under the skin of the object you are working on ". The only way for Matisse to find himself was to live in complete identification with all that nature could offer him. By identifying himself with

Portrait of Madame L.D., 1937   Pen and Indian Ink

nature, he acquired the right to observe her from a certain angle. So, however distant he seems from reality, it is no surprise to hear him say — " An attentive and respectful view of nature, and the duality of the feelings she has inspired in me, constitute my principal interest in art ". It was precisely this dual nature which contrasted the Matisse, a lover of the forms of nature, with the Matisse, carried away by a vision that tended to recreate them, forcing him to depict a world in which the illusions of imaginative thought and the tangible fruits of reality become confused.

It was Matisse himself, who, in about 1900 said that he had tried, literally, to copy faces from photographs, adding — " and it was this that kept me within what appeared to be the limits of the model's character. On occasions I have resorted to this method of working ".

No one would have found in work of this sort, a pointer towards the directions he was preparing to develop through so meticulous and scrupulous an attention to detail. It was later to lead him to the dazzling series of portraits of the Fauvist period *Woman with Hat, Margot, The Gipsy*, etc. and then to works in which his expression became more constructive — *Yvonne Landsberg, Greta Prozor, Head White and Rose* and *Madame L. D.* (Portrait Green, Blue, Yellow). He returned belatedly and not for long to them in 1947, with compositions so basically geometrical that they appear still to be influenced by Cubism. Each of these portraits illustrates with what masterly ease he was able to pass from one technique to another. But, in his own words, and in a letter to Henry Clifford, Conservator of the Philadelphia Museum, he wrote — " I have always tried to conceal my efforts ".

There is a series of portraits painted between 1909 and 1919 in which several artistic trends are grouped in a harmonious expression, as though they were produced separately. This series is situated between the period of violent coloration and draughtsmanship on the one hand, and the recent peaceful purging of what, without disparagement might be called the period of flat technique, when colour is stripped of all sense of relief. The capacity of Matisse to achieve a harmonious balance between draughtsmanship and the choice and application of colour, applies more particularly to his portraits. The intensity of a Fauvist is inherent in the economy of the use of colour in *Girl in a Green Dress* in which different methods are used and treatment is restrained. There is warmth of colour at one place in the picture only — the centre, in the depth of red of the flower on the corset. There is scarcely any relief on the face — only enough to attract our attention and to encourage us to search beyond the imperturbable calm, for some sign of character. *The Portrait of Madame Matisse* painted in 1913 (Musée de l'Hermitage, Leningrad) is in darker, grey-blue colours, not often employed by the artist. There is a trace of the ephemeral influence that Matisse received from Cézanne, which appeared again in the portrait of *Greta Prozor* in 1916. The grace and charm of attitude in this very fine portrait are obtained through a particular application of black in the line drawing which appears to emphasise the necessity for using this colour.

Matisse plumbed deeply the art of portraiture when he represented relief, later to be aban-

THE STRIPED DRESS, 1937 Oil
Norton Simon Collection, USA

◁

ELENA IN STRIPED DRESS, 1937 Oil 21 3/4″ × 11 3/4″
Mr and Mrs Alfred K. Stern Collection

STILL LIFE WITH OYSTERS, 1940
Oil 25³/₄″ × 32″ Museum of Art, Basel

STILL LIFE WITH MAGNOLIA, 1941
Oil $39\frac{1}{2}'' \times 28\frac{3}{4}''$ Musée National d'Art Moderne, Paris

doned in his portrait of *Marguerite Matisse*, also entitled *Head with Black Velvet* and dated 1916. It is now in a private collection. The colours employed, ochre, brown, red ochre and olive green, remain sober and eminently suitable to descriptive work. This is the one portrait in which Matisse claimed he had penetrated the mystery of expression and in which he insisted he had revealed his " almost religious feeling for life ".

MAGIC ARABESQUE

The aesthetic character of Matisse's conception of colour can readily be analysed. It is a great deal more difficult to understand his view of the form of objects. His choice of colour harmony seems often to have been based on the whims of his imagination, a desire to translate freely the delight of what he saw in a language whose strength lay in its very simplicity. Apart from an element of naïveté in his art, the techniques he employed in the application of colour have something in common with a typical child's picture. In recognising that " drawing is spiritual ", he further believed that it was the most intellectual and probably the most difficult element in his art to master for one who " wanted to be able to use colour as the vehicle for the expression of spiritual ideas ".

The reason why it is diffult to follow Matisse on the spiritual plane is because of the diversity of his means of expression. This became evident during the years following 1918, when he returned to the realist style. Incidentally, this reassured many art lovers and dealers who were disinclined to throw in their lot with new ideas in art. It comes as no surprise that this period coincided with confirmation of his success, raising the name of Matisse among the truly great contemporary painters. His canvases were now included in many more exhibitions. In 1919 he presented thirty-six works at Bernheim's and fifty-one at the Leicester Gallery in London. He exhibited at the Flechtheim Gallery in Berlin in 1921. He was now working with enthusiasm in his studio in the Ponchettes district of Nice, which he left only in 1938, when he stayed in a large apartment in the former Regina Hotel at Cimiez. Critics were now according him unstinted praise and the public called him " the painter of the *Odalisques* ". Important exhibitions of his works were held in 1924 in New York, Vienna, Copenhagen and Stockholm. He became a member of the Legion d'honneur in 1925 and gained the Carnegie Prize in 1927. He was now famous in spite of the fact that he had, in a few isolated pictures only, embarked on the style and technique that was to illustrate his outstanding personality.

Throughout this period and later on, the harmony between a careful observation of nature and rhythm in his composition in which his visual interpretation was often more important to him than the nature of his subject, dominated his work, which was executed with marked variation in technique. He observed the laws of classical perspective in these pictures, and the play of light and shade in his various ways of depicting relief. People were later to speak of Matisse's realism at this period compared with works painted before and after it.

THE BLACK DOOR
1942
Oil 24″ × 15″
Private
Collection

YOUNG GIRL IN WHITE ON A CHAISE-LONGUE, 1944
Oil 28 3/4″ × 23 1/2″   Private Collection

Matisse was never a spontaneous painter. He never felt the urge to improvise nor to be satisfied with a picture painted on the spur of the moment. He felt compelled to develop a subject by degrees, to paint by stages, producing successive versions all moving towards a more complete understanding of the whole. This occured more particularly around 1936, when he selected the technique of flat tints. He also developed a more intensive application of colour. His genius sprang from " long patience " and his bold style grew from leisurely study, the outcome of thoughtful development. " The impression of spontaneity comes when a painter's powers pass from the conscious to the unconscious state ". His words sum up the lines of his development.

The technique Matisse used in *Nude in Studio* and *Still Life with a Purro* illustrate how he translated methodically a subject into neo-Impressionist terms. His Fauvist style sometimes achieved the same end — *Young Sailor* painted at Collioure in 1906, with its passionate drawing, was but the second version of the same subject which had first been treated far more conventionally. Sometimes, without changing the style of a composition, he changed the dominant colour, as he did with the first version of *Harmony in Red* which was *Harmony in Blue*. Matisse painted twenty-six different pictures before completing the final version of *Pink Nude*. This system did not always succeed, for among the series of pictures preceding *Rumanian Blouse* there is one that appears to be far more successful than the final version. As the subject matter passed from one degree of simplification to the next, the draughtsmanship sometimes declined and as the fineness of the linework decreased, so the finished version took on a somewhat mediocre decorative motif. Matisse, however, took a contrary view. He once said — " When the picture springs immediately into shape, it becomes diagramatic, without substance and the expression suffers ".

With " realist " pictures, Matisse appears in an entirely different light. He is no longer concerned with painting, which becomes further simplified by stages in which colour did not mean simply " a vehicle for his emotion ". He came back to a realist view of the subject matter when he began painting his *Odalisques*, and created the idea that was to become an obsession and one of the underlying principles of his decorative art, the arabesque.

The origins of the pleasure he found in this art form are various, and are rooted in the past. Gustave Moreau might have been the first to attract the attention of Matisse to the rôle that Arabesque decoration can play in composition. Moreau often stressed the value of arabesque and mentioned it in his *Cahiers*. Matisse took considerable interest in the Exposition de l'Art Musulman at the Pavillion de Marsan in 1903 and later, in 1910, was equally interested in the Exposition de l'Art Islamique which he visited with Marquet. The East, as seen through the eyes of Islam, brought to Matisse a sense of refinement and a vision of the slow and meandering type of art, languid and voluptuous, rich in multi-coloured silks, ceramics and complicated ornaments.

The rhythm of the arabesque motif was an important element in Seurat's pictures, shown at the Salon des Indépendants in 1905 and particularly so in *Chahut* and *The Circus*. Matisse discovered this rhythm in a work of art in the same way as he did in anything that came

64

MICHAELLA, NICE, 1943
Oil 22³/₄″ × 27¹/₂″   Mrs Maurice Newton Collection, New York

"Tabac Royal" (Detail), 1943
Oil. Jacques Dubourg Collection, Paris

PINEAPPLE, 1948 Oil 45³/₄″ × 35″ Alex Hillmann Collection, New York

Composition with Standing Nude and Black Fern   Brush and Indian Ink

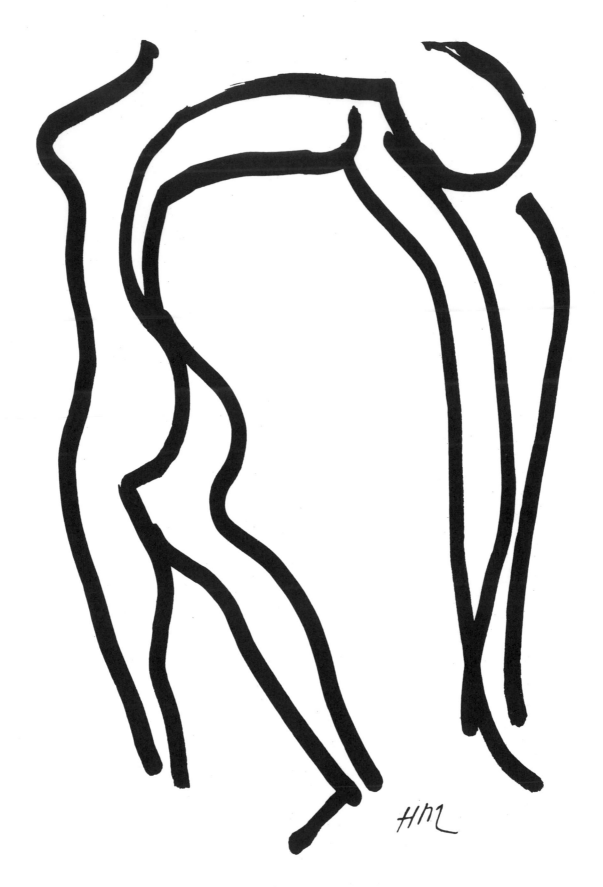

Dancer   Brush and Indian Ink

H.MATISSE 52

Blue Nude, 1952   Gouache on Cut and Pasted Paper   71

Portrait of Mademoiselle D. A., 1947 19″ × 12¹/₄″ Pencil

Self-Portrait with a Straw Hat, 1941   19″ × 14¹/₂″   Sanguine

NARCISSUS AND FRUIT, 1941   Oil 23 1/2" × 19 1/2"
Max Moos Collection, Geneva

H Matisse 43

Still Life Pen and Ink

75

Head of a Girl, 1942 Sanguine Drawing
Private Collection

visually to him. He wrote about Delacroix and Ingres in an article entitled " On colour " published in " Verve " No. 13, Vol. IV of 1945. " Both painters found a means of expression in the arabesque and in colour ". He had detected this common characteristic in the very different styles of the two painters just as he did with two others — " Gauguin and Van Gogh, later on, seem to have lived simultaneously in their arabesques and their colours ".

No one before Matisse had discovered so completely the association between colour and the arabesque motif, and illustrated them in a picture which brought to fruition a great deal of earlier experimentation, aiming at giving equal emphasis to the importance of the draughtsman's and colourist's contribution to art. From now onwards, they were to work each for the other, both able to preserve a measure of freedom of expression. Matisse might have repeated what Braque once said — " there is no confusion between form and colour — they synchronise ".

Before reaching the ultimate expression of his art and the refinement of the arabesque motif which, in some pictures had been no more than suggested, Matisse used a wide variety of decorative material such as stripes in cloth, carpet designs, porcelain ornamentation, embroidery on a dress and flowers on wallpaper. Detail in his motifs remained in character with the traditional conception of arabesque in the composition of a picture. Sometimes it took precedence over the main subject in the picture. This often occurred when Matisse appeared not to have come to a definite conclusion about the style to adopt. In such cases it is difficult to distinguish between realism and decoration, for Matisse tended sometimes to show a lack of decisiveness, and this may disappoint his admirers. In an article published in *La Grande Revue* of 1908, he wrote — " Composition can be defined as the art of arranging, in a decorative manner, the various elements that the painter can draw upon to express his feelings ". Many years later, in his conversations with André Verdet, he expressed his opinions on the future of painting along the lines he had adopted himself. " I think that, one day, the easel will disappear under the influence of changing conditions. Murals will replace it ".

The ambiguity resulting from two contradictory tendencies is illustrated in *Decorative*

Portrait of
Mademoiselle
M. A., 1942
Charcoal

Henri Matisse
2/42

Woman with Amphora, 1952
Gouache on Cut and Pasted Paper

figure on an ornamental background (Musée National d'Art Moderne, Paris) painted in 1927. The title suggests more a precise subject matter than the picture itself offers. The nude, seated on a carpet, facing a fruit dish, is not treated decoratively. The relief is expressed by ochre-coloured graded shadows similar to the lemons in the porcelain dish, with relief brought out through the effect produced by the lighting. But the nude which is the main subject of the picture, is of secondary importance on account of the extent of the ornamentation surrounding her, such as the stripes and oriental motifs of the carpet, large bunches of flowers on the mural hangings and the baroque frame of a mirror.

This is why Matisse was to upset completely the classical conception of the subject, which, throughout the history of art had meant the portrayal of a face, or in a still life, a group of objects against a background which, until then, had remained a relatively passive element in the picture. Its very unobtrusiveness often increased interest in the main subject of the picture. The classical rôle of the background was altered in most of Matisse's pictures; particularly so in several Odalisques and in works in flat tints of the 1935 period and up to the end of his life. The following canvases illustrate the point — *Woman with Red Jacket* (1937), *Still Life with Camelia* (1941), *Dancer Sitting on an Armchair* (1942), *Black Door* (1942), *Michaella* (1943), *Lute* (1943), *The Plum Tree Branch* (1948).

In all these pictures, there is no variation of interest or emphasis thoughout the canvas. Vases, bunches of flowers, furniture, ornaments, wallpaper and carpets are all treated with equal emphasis to the figures which seem to be of limited interest to the painter, individually; though each possesses a character to be revealed. Their faces lack expression and are sometimes of no importance whatsoever. They are nothing more than forms to be added to the arabesque decor, anonymous splashes of colour whose only justification is that of participating in the overall harmony and rhythm of the picture.

The transition from so personal a style of painting to the technique of the juxtaposition of coloured paper as an art form, caused no apparent change in Matisse's appreciation of art. On abandoning the outline round the subject matter, it became clear that the artist was now " drawing " with a pair of scissors. He wrote — " there is no break in the continuity between my previous pictures and my cuttings. All that has happened is that I have penetrated through to the essential and abstract nature of forms and I have preserved the subject which, formerly, I had presented in too complex a manner. It is necessary, now, to gain a clear notion of the main subject and its association with other less essential matter ". Matisse embarked on coloured paper cuttings for the first time in 1930, for the rough draft of his great mural painting on the theme of *The Dance* for the Barnes Foundation at Merion, in the United States. Later, when he was immobilised through illness in 1941 and was unable to paint, he adopted this technique as a new art form. Of this, he once said — " to cut from the living colour has something in common with a sculptor's trimming his stone". Matisse was now between seventy and eighty years of age. He was eighty-four in 1953 when he did his last cuttings of gouache and he died the following year. The ageing Matisse was astonishingly vigorous for his years. There was great decision in his choice of a form, there was movement and rhythm in his compositions, gaiety in his arrangement of colour, adding weight to the notion that he had reached the apotheosis of his art in the final manifestations of his genius.

Nevertheless, the final stage was one of pure decoration and illustration and was a work of limited importance. The book *Jazz*, written and illustrated by him and reproduced very faithfully in stencil form (Tériade 1947) was one of the most successful exam-

Woman with Amphora, 1952
Gouache on Cut and Pasted Paper

79

ples of this process. It was completed between 1945 and 1947. He wrote — " These pictures in bright and violent colours are the quintessence of my memories of the circus, legends and journeys ". The fauna and flora appearing in his cuttings were also reminiscent of his long stay in Tahiti in 1930. Altogether, they represent an enrichment of his conception of arabesque decoration. Outstanding amongst them is the series of great *Blue Nudes*, in monochrome, of 1952, in which he achieved a purity of expression most economically and without any loss of sensibility.

MATISSE, DRAUGHTSMAN AND SCULPTOR

A glance at one of his works shows how much importance Matisse attached to draughtsmanship despite the fact that in most of his paintings, he employed a very noticeable and often black outline. For him, drawing was a passion, but a passion that worried him and made considerable demands upon him. In his painting, he tried to reconcile a scrupulously fair view of life, aesthetically portrayed, which was to lead him, step by step, towards a reconstruction of the various elements in a complete work of art. In his old age, he found that by drawing, he could restore his strength. He was over eighty when, unable to leave his room at Cimiez owing to an illness, he came to realise that the ceiling above his bed was as white as the surface of paper. He attached a piece of charcoal to the end of a fishing rod and began to draw figures on the ceiling in an effort to combat his idleness.

The many drawings he left behind illustrate the complexity of his artistic evolution. Apart from his studio work, initial studies and exercises in technique, his drawings of all sorts in pencil, charcoal or ink may be divided into two main classes. Those that are realistic and resemble the object, and those in which a calculated deformation appears, the result of careful thought in the abstract. The realist group contains some fine nudes, lifelike portraits such as those of the Cone sisters, Claribel and Etta, who possessed an important Matisse Collection of forty-two paintings, eighteen sculptures and one hundred and fourteen drawings now in the Baltimore Museum. There are also the humorous self-portraits and the whole series of drawings of his model Antoniette who posed for the famous *White Plumes*. Of the two distinct techniques, it is clear that he revealed his great originality in his schematic drawings. Matisse was often able to express character and grace by means of a single, essential and flexible line, drawn with consummate skill. His standard was so high that he could not hope to repeat it on all occasions; but his feminine forms, a face, a hand holding a flowering branch, a bunch of flowers in a vase, or simply a coffee cup on a saucer, undoubtedly show he wished to avoid any trace of virtuosity.

On other occasions, Matisse translated into sign language the shape of a face, a body or some fruit, by a stroke with a brush dipped in Indian ink. These drawings might appear to have been made nonchalantly, but in his own words — " an object must be studied for a long time before one can reproduce its symbol ". His constructive mind was for ever

PIERROT'S FUNERAL   Gouache on Cut and Pasted Paper for the Book "Jazz" by Henri Matisse (Tériade, Paris 1947)

bent on controlling the free movement of his impulsive hand. " I have always been greatly helped by the use I have made of a lead weight on a string. The vertical has always helped me to calculate the direction of a line and in my quick sketches when I am at work on a branch of a tree in the country, I do not draw a curve without studying it in relation to the vertical. My curves are not drawn wildly " (*Jazz*).

Matisse made his first lithographs in 1904. He developed his art slowly and patiently. Whatever it was, relief minutely expressed, a line precisely tracing the contours, apparently done with an etching needle, all gradually became important elements in his drawings. His best illustrations for books were lithographs: *Les Visages* by Pierre Reverdy (Ed. du Chêne, 1946), les *Lettres de la religieuse portugaise* (Tériade, 1946) and, in particular, *Florilège des Amours de Ronsard* (Skira, 1948), and *Poèmes* by Charles d'Orléans. There were, also, his nudes, mermaids, faces of women and flowers drawn as simple lines from the point of a coloured pencil, and they represent the finest, the most serene examples of graphic art by Matisse. He used etchings to illustrate some books (*Poésies* by Stéphane Mallarmé, *Ulysses* by James Joyce) and less frequently woodcuts (*Les Fleurs du Mal* by Baudelaire). Matisse worked on many other art forms such as cartoons for tapestries (*The Woman with a Lute, Papeete, Nymph and Satyr*), ceramics (*Saint Dominique* in the church at the Plateau d'Assy) and stained glass. His outstanding architectural and decorative contribution which involved every aspect of his creative genius concerned the building of the Chapelle du Rosaire at Vence, consecrated on 25th June, 1951. He contributed to the preparation of the plans, prepared designs for the stalls and doors, designed the mural ceramics, crosses and candelabra and the vestments. He also created the colours of the stained glass through which bright, warm sunlight spreads across the interior of the chapel. In a message addressed to his native town of Cateau at the inauguration of the Musée Matisse in 1952, he said — " It was as a result of the creation of the chapel at Vence that I finally found myself ". Of all his artistic output, Matisse considered this work as his finest contribution. Finally, at the close of this brief study of the many facets of the artistic wealth possessed by Matisse, there is Matisse, the sculptor. He was thirty-one when he began to take a serious interest in sculpture in the year 1900, while attending evening classes at the Ecole Municipale in the rue Etienne-Marcel. He had previously done a little modelling and produced *Jaguar Devouring a Hare*, inspired by a bronze of Barye. His interest in sculpture originated as a result of the visit he paid in 1897 to Rodin's studio. He became impressed by the great power and freedom of Rodin's expression. The first sculpted female bust by Matisse, a statuette entitled *The Slave*, was influenced by Rodin and by Bourdelle whose classes he was following then at the Grande-Chaumière. Later, the series of figurines (*Madeleine, Seated Nude with Arms behind Head*), completed between 1901 and 1906 bear the stamp of Matisse's style and take their place in the history of sculpture in the early years of the twentieth century. The aesthetic distortions that later sculptors developed further and more systematically, originated with Matisse. In sculpture, Matisse appears more revolutionary than in his style of painting at the same period. *Heads of Jeannette*, completed

à Monique Mercier
Son admirateur
H Matisse 51

Portrait of Mademoiselle Monique Mercier, 1951   Brush and Indian Ink

YOUNG ENGLISH
GIRL, 1947
Oil 21 8/4″ × 13″
Private Collection

PLUM TREE BRANCH WITH GREEN BACKGROUND, 1948   Oil 45$\frac{3}{4}$″ × 35″
Mrs Albert D. Lasker Collection, New York

Self-Portrait of Matisse   Pencil Drawing
Musée Matisse, Nice

between 1910 and 1913 are a fine example of his personality in three dimensional art.

In sculpture as in painting, Matisse did not confine himself to a single aesthetic style. Instead of producing richly ornamented mouldings, he was sometimes satisfied with simple polished surfaces. He even returned to a more classical view of forms as in the third version of his *Large Head* of 1929, also called *Henriette*.

He was an active and regular sculptor for some thirty years and returned to it in later life. His *Standing Nude* (or *Katia*) of 1950 and the crucifix for the chapel at Vence are examples of his later work. His total output was not very great, amounting to some seventy bronzes in all. Apart from some outstanding work, the general impression he left behind him is one of instability, suggesting that he felt powerless to solve three dimensional problems. His usual reticence when confronted with technical aptitude and his distrust for ready-made results in sculpture did not always combine to produce a happy result. It is difficult to gain a clear picture of his aims when he undertook a type of work in which he was unable to make use of colour, that exciting tool of his trade that facinated him throughout his life. But since he used colour so as to do away with all notions of volume, perhaps he found some compensation in giving himself up to the one joy, that of creating forms. These were often inspired by his pictures or were forerunners of forms that were later to appear, such as *Seated Nude, with Back Turned* which had already appeared in *Les Demoiselles à la Rivière* or in *Reclining Nude*, of 1928, so similar to *Blue Nude* of 1907. Matisse was never forthcoming, himself, as regards his own sculpture. During a talk with Georges Charbonnier (*Le Monologue du peintre*, Julliard, 1960) he simply said — "I did my sculpture as a painter. I did not work as a sculptor".

A PAINTER'S PHILOSOPHY

It may surprise some people to read Guillaume Apollinaire's view of Matisse in 1907 at the height of the Fauvist period. " The characteristic of the art of Matisse is that of being reasonable". So lucid a remark would, today, seem prophetic; for it applied more to the painter's future. Matisse, himself, was later to confirm this opinion in an article published in *La Grande Revue* of 25th December, 1908. " I dream of an art transfusing a sense of balance, purity and calm, in which there is no discordant or worrying note, available for all who use their minds, for the businessman as well as the lettered artist, a balm, a means of calming the spirit, something similar to a comfortable armchair which brings refreshment to physical tiredness ".

It is clear that there is no discordant note, no metaphysical or poetical disturbance in Matisse's works of art. His paintings are not a mirror in which doubts and anxieties are reflected. For him, painting was the embodiment of an ideal universe, obliterating the world around us and reminding us of it only when we need a glimpse of reality to

Lithography for " Florilège des Amours de Ronsard " (Albert Skira, Paris 1948)

calm us. In this respect, Matisse was, decidedly a painter of illusions.

Optimistic expressions such as " life through rose-coloured spectacles " and " seeing things in their best light " apply perfectly to what Matisse considered his art should accomplish. His great merit was that he added style to gaiety. He transformed happiness by making it interesting. Gide might have appeared surprised to see from " worthy sentiments " the emergence of good painting.

Matisse strove to produce a peaceful and colourful world. Although he always enlivened his paintings with baroque-like movement, there was never any trace of human agitation. His was, rather, a mobile world seen through a passive, contemplative eye. Humanity described or called to mind by Matisse is a restful humanity. The characters he brings to life are enclosed between four walls making use of the furniture the painter has to draw upon: beds, couches, chaises-longue, armchairs and sometimes, carpets. Lying, sitting or crouching, his womenfolk take up attitudes of oriental idleness. It is, for ever, springtime or summer. Flowering branches have just been gathered in the garden and the sun is, for ever, shining. The window is always open so that we can all rejoice in company with the artist. Sometimes, the shutters are closed against the hot noonday sun and it is cool and shady within.

Madame L. D. Portrait Green, Blue and Yellow, 1947   Oil   Private Collection

Drawing in Indian Ink with Brush

CREOLE DANCER
1950
Gouache on Cut
and Pasted Paper
$80^{3}/_{4}'' \times 47^{1}/_{4}''$
Musée Matisse
Nice

ZULMA, 1950
Gouache on Cut
and Pasted Paper
$92\frac{1}{2}" \times 57"$
Royal Museum
of Fine Art
Copenhagen

H. MATISSE
50

Matisse gave birth to an active, intense life enclosed within the silent, motionless world of art which Claudel said we could " hear " with our eyes. But life expressed by Matisse is no different to the life we feel within ourselves, revealed to us at moments of ecstacy; when elation, radiating around us brightens everything within range. Matisse conveys a passionate love of life through the active, insistent rôle of colour in art, carrying us beyond ourselves and beyond the world around us. Colour is the music accompanying the silent scenes from opera played before us within countless little magic theatres. There is but one theme — the exploration of gay, illusory and untravelled worlds without substance. The measureless, colourful universe, bathed in the light of the constant sun brings back a measure of joy to us, the spectators. Once within and guided by the sure hand of the painter, our whole selves are transformed by an all-embracing sense of vision. Liberated and enriched by colour, emerging and fading in kaleidoscopic brilliance, we feel moved to repeat what Apollinaire wrote in a preface towards the end of his life, half a century ago. " His art lies open and revealed. In spite of the ever-growing simplicity of its form, it has not failed, in its development, to become even more magnificent ".

BIOGRAPHY

1869. Henri Matisse born at Cateau (Nord) on 31st December.

1887-1888. First visit to Paris as a law student.

1889. A barrister's clerk at Saint-Quentin, Matisse studied drawing at the Ecole Quentin-Latour.

1890. Matisse painted his first pictures.

1892. Matisse moved to Paris and studied at the Ecole des Arts Décoratifs. He worked at the Académie Julian in Bouguereau's studio and finally with Gabriel Ferrier. He was not accepted for the entrance examination to L'Ecole des Beaux-Arts.

1895. Gustave Moreau accepted Matisse in his studio at the Beaux-Arts. Matisse spent a short period in Brittany.

1896. Pictures by Matisse shown for the first time at the Salon de la Société des Beaux-Arts. He spent his holidays at Belle-Ile.

1897. Matisse spent the summer at Belle-Ile.

1898. On 8th January he married Amélie Alexandrine Parayre. Honeymoon spent in London. He spent the winter in Corsica followed by a visit to the Toulouse region. He left the Beaux-Arts after Moreau's death.

1899. Matisse worked at the Carrière Studio.

1900. He worked with Marquet on decorations at the Grand Palais for L'Exposition Universelle.

1901. First pictures by Matisse shown at the Salon des Indépendants. He paid a visit to Switzerland.

1902. Paintings by Matisse exhibited at Berthe Weill Gallery.

1903. Exhibitions at the Druet Gallery and the Salon d'Automne.

1904. The first private exhibition at Vollard's Gallery. The summer spent at Saint-Tropez. Matisse met Signac and Cross. First neo-Impressionist paintings.

1905. The summer spent at Collioure with Derain. The first Fauvist paintings by Matisse shown at the Salon d'Automne.

1906. His second private exhibition at Druet's Gallery. The spring spent at Biskera, the summer at Collioure.

1907. Matisse in Italy.

1908. He visited Germany. Exhibitions of work by Matisse in New York, London, Stockholm, Moscow and Berlin.

1909. Matisse collaborated in work at "la Toison d'Or" in Moscow.

1910. Sixty-six of Matisse's paintings exhibited at the Bernheim-Jeune Gallery. He stayed at Munich with Marquet and later travelled in Spain.

1911. Several exhibitions of Matisse's work abroad. He travelled to Moscow.

1912. Matisse visited Morocco.

1913. Second visit to Morocco. Several exhibitions of his work in Europe and in the U.S.A.

1914. Matisse is invalided out of the army. He stayed at Collioure with Marquet and Juan Gris.

1915. Exhibitions of Matisse's work at New York.

1916. Exhibition in London. Matisse stayed at Nice.

1917. Summer spent in Touraine. He moved to Nice.

1918. Matisse exhibited at Paul Guillaume's gallery with Picasso.

1919. Thirty-six of his pictures exhibited at the Bernheim Gallery and fifty-one at the Leicester Gallery in London.

1920. The summer spent at Etretat. In London, he created the décor for *Rossignol* by Strawinsky for the Diaghilev Ballet.

1924. Exhibitions in New York, Vienna, Copenhagen, Stockholm and Paris.

1925. Trip to Italy. Matisse received the Légion d'Honneur. He exhibited at the Tate Gallery in London.

1927. Matisse received the Carnegie Prize. Exhibitions in New York, Glasgow and Paris.

1930. Matisse spent the summer months in Tahiti. Exhibition in Berlin. He travelled to the U.S.A. in the autumn.

1931. Matisse at Nice. Exhibitions at the Basel Museum and the Museum of Modern Art in New York.

1933. Matisse at Merion (U.S.A.) for the mural décor (*La Danse*) at the Barnes Foundation. Visit to Italy. Matisse does etchings to illustrate Malarmé's *Poésies*.

1935. Etchings for Joyce's *Ulysses*. Cartoons for tapestries.

1936. Exhibitions at San Francisco and at Paul Rosenberg Gallery in Paris.

1938. Matisse moved to the old Regina Hotel at Cimiez. He completed the décor and costumes for *Rouge et Noir* by Chostakovitch for the Ballets Russes of Monte-Carlo.

1939. Matisse in Paris in the summer. The autumn spent at Cimiez.

1941. Matisse fell ill and began coloured paper cuttings.

1943. He moved to the villa "Le Rêve" at Vence.

1945. His works exhibited at the Salon d'Autumn.

1947. Matisse made Commandeur de la Légion d'Honneur.

1948. Matisse worked on the mural painting for the Church of Our Lady at Toute Grace at Plateau d'Assy. He worked until 1951 on the building and decoration of the Chapelle des Dominicaines de Monteils at Vence.

1949. Exhibitions at the Pierre Matisse Gallery in New York and at the Musée National d'Art Moderne in Paris. Exhibitions of his work at Lucerne.

1950. An exhibition at the Maison de la Pensée Française in Paris.

1951. Exhibitions in Tokyo, in Germany and in several cities in the U.S.A.

1952. The Musée Matisse at Cateau opened.

1954. Henri Matisse died at Cimiez on 3rd November.

1956. An important exhibition of his works at the Musée National d'Art Moderne in Paris.

BIBLIOGRAPHY
PRINCIPAL MONOGRAPHS

SCHACHT, Roland. *Henri Matisse*. R. Kæmmerer, Dresden, 1922. Quarto.

BASLER, Adolphe. *Henri Matisse*. Junge Kunst, Leipzig, 1924.

FELS, Florent. *Henri Matisse*. Paris, 1929. Quarto.

BERTRAM, Antony. *Matisse*. The World's Masters. London, 1930.

FRY, Roger. *Henri Matisse*. E. Weyhe, New York, 1930 Quarto.

COURTHION, Pierre. *Henri Matisse*. Rieder, Paris, 1934.

KAWASHIMA, R. *Matisse*. Tokyo, 1936.

ESCHOLIER, Raymond. *Henri Matisse*. Floury, Paris, 1937.

CASSOU, Jean. *Matisse*. Braun, Paris, 1939.

ROGER-MARX, Claude. *Dessins de Henri Matisse*, Braun, Paris, 1939. Small in folio.

COURTHION, Pierre. *Le Visage de Matisse*. Marguerat, Lausanne, 1943.

ARAGON, Louis. *Matisse : dessins, thèmes et variations*. Fabiani, Paris, 1943. Quarto.

GRUNEWALD, Isaac. *Matisse och Expressionismen*. W. Wildstrand, Stockholm, 1944.

SWANE, Leo. *Henri Matisse*. P. A. Nordstedt, Stockholm, 1944.

WALSESCHI, Marco. *Disegni di Henri Matisse*. Hoepli, Milan, 1944.

Matisse. De la couleur. "Verve", vol. IV. No. 13. Paris, 1945.

ARAGON. Louis. *Apologie du Luxe*. Skira, Geneva, 1946. In folio.

LEJARD, André. *Matisse. Peintures 1939-1946*. Ed. du Chêne, Paris, 1946.

SCHEIWILLER, Giovanni. *Henri Matisse*. Hoepli, Milan, 1947.

Matisse. Vence 1944-1948 "Verve", vol. VI, No. 21-22, Paris, 1948.

LEJARD, André. *Matisse*. Hazan, Paris, 1948.

MALINGUE, Maurice. *Matisse, Dessins*. Ed. des Deux Mondes, Paris, 1949.

BARR JR., Alfred H. *Matisse. His Art and His public*. The Museum of Modern Art, New York, 1951. Quarto.

VERDET, André. *Prestiges de Matisse*. Emile-Paul, Paris, 1952.

HUYGHE, René. *Matisse*. Flammarion ("Le Grand Art en Livres de Poche"), Paris, 1953.

GREENBERG, Clement. *Henri Matisse*. Harry N. Abrams New York, 1953.

DIEHL, Gaston. *Henri Matisse*. Pierre Tisné, Paris, 1954. Quarto.

LIEBERMAN, William S. *Matisse, 50 years of his graphic art*. George Braziller, New York, 1956. Quarto.

ESCHOLIER, Raymond. *Matisse, ce vivant*. A. Fayard, Paris, 1956. 12c.

LASSAIGNE, Jacques. *Matisse*. Skira, Geneva, 1959.

BOOKS ILLUSTRATED BY MATISSE

LES JOCKEYS CAMOUFLÉS, by *Pierre Reverdy*. Drawings. A la Belle Edition, Paris, 1918. Octavo.

CINQUANTE DESSINS. Préface by *Charles Vildrac*. Published by the artist. Paris, 1920. Small in-folio.

POÉSIES, by *Stéphane Mallarmé*. Etchings. Skira, Lausanne, 1932. Quarto.

ULYSSES, by *James Joyce*. Etchings. New York, 1935.

PASIPHAÉ, by *Henry de Montherlant*. Linos. Fabiani, Paris, 1944.

LETTRES DE LA RELIGIEUSE PORTUGAISE. Lithos. Tériade, Paris, 1946.

VISAGES, by *Pierre Reverdy*. Lithos. Edition du Chêne, Paris, 1946.

REPLI, by *André Rouveyre*. Lithos. Edition du Bélier, Paris, 1947.

LES FLEURS DU MAL, by *Charles Baudelaire*. Etchings, wood-cuts and photo-lithos. La Bibliothèque française, Paris, 1947.

JAZZ, by *Henri Matisse*. Stencils from original cuttings. Tériade, Paris, 1947. Quarto (large).

LES MIROIRS PROFONDS. Poems and drawings. Maeght, Paris, 1947. Quarto.

LE VENT DES EPINES, by *Jacques Kobler*. Drawings by Matisse, Bonnard, Braque. Maeght, Paris, 1947. Quarto.

FLORILÈGE DES AMOURS DE RONSARD. Lithos. Skira, Paris, 1948. Quarto.

MIDIS GAGNÉS, by *Tristan Tzara*. Drawings. Denoël, Paris, 1948.

POÈMES, by *Charles d'Orléans*. Lithos in colour. Tériade, Paris, 1950. In-folio.

ILLUSTRATIONS